Passive Income

Stop working - Start living - Make money while you sleep

By Ralph Waters

Table of Contents

Introduction

Do you dream about achieving true financial freedom? Do you want more time to spend with your family and friends, or to do the things you love?

Money does make certain aspects of life easy. It makes it possible to do things we couldn't do without it. We could all use more money than we have. For many of us, it can seem like the only way to get it is to put in longer hours at work than we already do. We feel limited in terms of what we can earn. Taking a second (or third) job is exhausting to think about, yet many people do exactly that in an effort to break free of debt and earn a good income.

There's an old adage that says that nobody ever wishes, on their deathbed, that they had spent more time working. Whatever you earn during your lifetime – and however much time you spend earning it – you can't take it with you when your life is over.

Working longer hours, and taking time away from the people and things you love, is not the answer. The real answer is to find ways to make money that are reliable and steady, and that don't require you to spend your life working so hard that you don't have time to smell the roses.

What You Will Learn in This Book

What if you could earn money while you sleep, or while you spend quality time with your family and friends? The goal of this book is to help you do exactly that. It might sound too good to be true – but I promise you, it's not. The secret to accomplishing that goal is learning about a type of income called passive income.

In the first chapter, I will cover the basics of passive income. What is it, and how does it differ from the income you earn working a 9-to-5 job? I'll give you basic definitions of active and passive income so that you understand the difference – and why passive income is preferable to active income in the long run. I'll also explain why it is so important to set up multiple sources of passive income if you want to attain true financial freedom.

The second chapter will go a little deeper into the benefits and risks of passive income. Any income strategy, no matter how tempting or reliable it sounds, carries some risk. That is inevitable, and it is important to understand those risks before you move forward. In my opinion, the benefits of earning passive income far outweigh the risks. However, you need to make that decision for yourself, and the information in this chapter will help you do so. I'll also give you an overview of my favorite methods of earning passive income, which I will explore in greater depth in the coming chapters.

In the third chapter, I will talk about one of my favorite passive income methods: writing an eBook. It might seem like a daunting task to write a book, but I'll give you my best tips on how to get it accomplished. We'll talk about making the decision to write the book yourself, as well as the option of hiring a professional ghostwriter to do it for you. I'll include tips for hiring a ghostwriter, and how to find a designer to create a compelling cover for your book. I'll also cover the process of formatting your book to sell on the Kindle store, writing a book description that will help your book sell, and uploading the book using Amazon KDP. Finally, I'll tell you how to market your book using specialty websites, social media, and more.

In the fourth chapter, I'll talk in detail about marketing affiliate products. Affiliate products are often the first thing that people new to the idea of earning money online try, and yet they often fail. I'll help you understand the process, starting with choosing a niche and researching the competition, as well as giving you tips on how to choose the best affiliate products to guarantee a stream of passive income. After that, I'll tell you how to set up a website using WordPress and how to optimize your site so that it ranks high on Google. Finally, I'll give you some tips for obtaining quality backlinks to boost your rank, and tell you how to market your products on social media.

The fifth chapter covers several other methods of earning passive income. Writing eBooks and selling affiliate products are my favorite methods, and so I have covered those in a lot of depth because they are my areas of expertise. However, I do want you to be aware that there are many other methods you can use to earn passive income. In this last chapter, I will cover numerous methods, including:

- How to conceptualize, create, and sell a mobile app. Mobile apps are more popular than ever. While coming up with an idea for a great app isn't easy, I'll give you some pointers on how to do it.

- How to set up and monetize a YouTube channel, including information about creating and promoting your videos, and using YouTube to boost your SEO.

- How to create and sell an online course in your area of expertise. If you feel that you have the knowledge and passion to teach others about something, the time and effort involved with creating a course might be worth the effort. I'll also give you some information about where and how to sell your course.

- How to conceptualize and create your own product. Selling affiliate products is easy, and selling your own product is a way of taking what you learn from affiliate marketing to the next level. When you create a great product, you can earn a significant profit from it. I'll even explain the benefits of setting up your own program to let affiliates do the marketing for you.

- Niche product review sites are very popular, and I'll explain how to take your affiliate marketing skills and use them in a different way by reviewing and comparing products within a niche.

By the time you are done reading this book, you will have all of the information you need to start building multiple passive income streams, and be well on your way to true financial freedom.

Let's get started.

Chapter 1: Understanding Passive Income

The first step is to understand what passive income is and how it differs from the kind of income you earn working an hourly or salaried job. The differences are key because they point the way to financial freedom. If you want to be your own boss and the master of your own destiny, passive income is the way to do it.

The Differences between Active and Passive Income

Even if you use a different term to describe it, you already know what active income is. Active income is the kind of income that requires you to actively engage in work for a set period of time before you earn it. For example, if you have a job that pays you by the hour, you receive money only for the hours you work – right? That's active income because your activity is required on a consistent basis if you want to earn a living.

The same is true of a job where you earn a salary. You are expected to do certain work in exchange for your salary. You must show up at work on time, work a set number of hours, and complete the duties that are part of your job description in order to earn your salary. You may even be required to work additional hours without additional pay if you are an employee with exempt status.

Finally, freelance work also qualifies as active income. Freelance workers get paid only for the work they complete. If they get sick and are unable to complete a task or job, they earn nothing.

Now let's contrast that with passive income. Passive income is income that may require some work to set up. However, once you have established a passive income stream, it often requires only minimum maintenance to keep the money flowing.

Let's look at a simple example. If you write an eBook, you must spend time and energy writing it. You have to hire an editor and someone to design the book's cover, and you'll have to make sure that it's in the proper format to sell on Amazon. However, once the book is completed and it's for sale on Amazon's website, you will earn money every time someone buys the book. That's what makes the income passive. If someone buys a copy while you're on vacation or asleep, you still earn money.

I hope you are beginning to see why passive income is the answer to achieving financial freedom. Instead of adding more hours to your workday, passive income can make it possible for you to work fewer hours and still earn a living.

Why Passive Income Matters

Now let's talk about why having sources of passive income is so important. The average person is not going to earn a huge salary. True, a select few people do earn enormous salaries as CEOs or in other top executive positions. Others may be in-demand consultants who can charge huge hourly rates. For the majority of us, though, our income potential is not huge. We are limited by our education, experience, and the number of hours that we can physically (and mentally) spare for work.

Passive income opens up possibilities that might not otherwise exist. It allows us to earn money in ways that do not require hours of additional effort on an ongoing basis – and that's huge. If you find that working long hours translates to having only a limited amount of time with your family – or that you're passing up opportunities to do what you love – then passive income can make the difference.

Passive income matters because it's the kind of income that can easily supplement your active income – and eventually, it may even replace your active income. Your earnings with active income are limited based on the number of hours you work, as well as by things like your education and work history. There are no such limitations on passive income. You have complete control over it, which means that nobody can cap it. The fact that you can earn it while you are sleeping, playing with your kids, or on the golf course means that you have the freedom to do what you please with your time.

As you can see, passive income does differ significantly from active income. Money is money, but the money you earn from passive income streams is the kind of money that can set you free from the daily grind and allow you to pursue the things that are most important to you.

In the next chapter, we will talk about the benefits and risks of passive income in greater detail so that you know what to expect as you work toward setting up passive income streams.

Chapter 2: The Possibilities of Passive Income

Before I share the best ways to earn passive income with you, I want to take a few pages to review the benefits and risks of passive income. The truth is that no form of income is without risk. Even if you were fortunate enough to inherit a large amount of money, there would be some risk involved with investing it. That's the way life works.

We have already touched on some of the benefits of passive income, but let's review them in a bit more depth:

1. Passive income can lead to financial freedom. When you earn passive income, you can earn it any time of day or night, and from anywhere in the world. You do not have to be tied to a particular job or schedule. Once your passive income streams are set up, the money will flow into your account.

2. There is no limit on passive income. There is nothing preventing you from setting up a hundred different streams of passive income if you choose to do so. You can dedicate as much time as you wish to establishing pas-

sive income streams, and once they are set up you can sit back and collect the money. You are not limited by the number of hours you work.

3. Passive income can come from a variety of sources, which means that you can choose the options that appeal to you the most. You aren't limited or required to do work that you genuinely dislike. You have the ability to choose work that you love.

4. You can be your own boss. When you set up passive income streams, you don't have to answer to anybody other than yourself. You can decide when to work and when not to work. You set your own hours, and you can decide the best way to do things without interference from anybody else.

In my opinion, those are some very good benefits – and reason enough to take the time and energy to set up passive income streams. However, there are some risks and concerns to address too.

1. Setting up passive income streams takes time and effort. It might be tempting to look at passive income streams as easy and requiring little labor. However, that is an overly simplistic view and one that can lead to misunderstandings down the line. Make no mistake. You are going to have to dedicate a

significant amount of time – and probably invest some money, too – if you want to get your passive income streams up and flowing. All passive income is active at the beginning.

2. Passive income streams don't grow overnight. Even if you put in a lot of effort, it may take a while for passive income to become a stream. In fact, it may start off feeling more like a series of inconsequential drips than a true stream. You need to be prepared for the eventuality that it will take some time to get things flowing. That's one of the reasons that I recommend starting to set up your passive streams before you quit your day job.

3. You need to diversify to ensure that you have money flowing in at all times. A single stream of passive income is not going to be enough to help you achieve financial security and freedom. The danger is that your stream could dry up, leaving you with no income at all. The best way to overcome this particular risk is to set up multiple streams of income so that even if one source slows down, you'll have others in place that are still bringing you money.

4. Passive income can be too passive for some people. It's a very rare person who will feel passionate and fulfilled about income

streams that require little or no work. No matter what you choose to do, it's probably best to combine some active work that fulfills and satisfies you – even if it doesn't pay much – with passive income streams to help you earn money.

In my opinion, the benefits of setting up passive income streams far outweigh the risks. Passive income, as I said, starts out active. As long as you are prepared to do the work to make those streams flow, then passive income could be the best way for you to achieve financial freedom.

Proven Passive Income Strategies

As I mentioned in the introduction, the next three chapters will cover some of my favorite passive income strategies in depth. There are many different ways to earn passive income, and you certainly do not need to restrict yourself to the methods I discuss here. However, these methods are, I believe, some of the most reliable and easy to achieve.

Here is a quick overview so you know what to expect in the coming chapters.

- Writing an eBook is the first method I will cover. A lot of people get intimidated by the idea of writing an eBook because they don't consider themselves to be writers. I will cover the topic in great depth, and explain how you can get a book written with relative ease, and market it effectively. A well-written eBook can easily earn you income for the rest of your life.

- Marketing affiliate products is the second topic I will cover. Affiliate products tend to get a bad rap because a lot of people try to market them and don't earn any money. The reason they fail to earn money is not because affiliate marketing is bad – it's because they don't go about it the right way. I'll tell you how to choose the best products, and set up your revenue streams so that they require little ongoing work from you.

- Creating a mobile app is another popular way of creating passive income. There are a lot of apps out there, but if you can come up with a unique one, you can sell it for years without having to do any additional work. You don't even need to be a programmer to create an app.

- YouTube is one of the world's most-trafficked websites and a great source of passive income if you know how to use it. I'll explain how to set up a YouTube channel, give you tips for creating videos, and tell you how to monetize and publicize your videos.

- Creating an online course is in some ways the most labor-intensive of all the options here, but it is also a very good way to earn significant passive income. I'll give you tips for choosing a topic, creating a course, setting a price, and marketing your course.

- In case affiliate marketing isn't enough for you, I'll talk about the benefits of creating your own product to sell, and how you can set up your own affiliate programs.

- Product review and comparison sites are very popular, and I'll give you some pointers about how to take affiliate marketing to a new level.

The next three chapters will go into great depth on these topics so that you have all of the tools you need to do what you need to do. You do not need to use all of these methods to attain financial freedom. What I recommend is that you read everything, and start with the method that most appeals to you first. Once you have done the work necessary to establish a stream of passive income, you can choose another method – or repeat the first one. It is certainly possible to earn money by writing multiple eBooks, or by setting up a string of affiliate websites.

The most important thing to remember is that you do not want to put all of your financial eggs into one basket. The point of having passive income is that you want to be able to spend your time doing the things you love. If you have multiple streams of income, it won't have a significant impact on you if one stream suddenly slows down or dries up. True financial freedom means that you do not have to rely on a single source of income.

Chapter 3: Writing an eBook

I want to start with one of my favorite methods of earning passive income, writing an eBook. It used to be that getting a book published required a great deal of effort. Writers had to first write the book – or write a detailed book proposal. Then they had to send out query letters to agents and publishers in the hopes that what they had written would resonate with someone. Even getting a book agent to read your letter was an uphill battle. Most agents were inundated with thousands of letters from aspiring authors. Both luck and talent were required in order for an author to get noticed.

I think it's important to be honest about the amount of work required to write and publish an eBook. Passive income does not start out passive. You must put in the work up front. Once the stream of income is established, it becomes passive. If you decide to write an eBook yourself, it may takes months to complete the writing depending on your writing speed and ability. Even if you hire a ghostwriter, the process can take a while and will require some thought and effort from you.

Finding a Niche for Your eBook

Let's start with the very important first step: choosing a niche for your eBook. If you plan on writing the book yourself, it is probably best to choose a niche and topic that interest you, and about which you have some knowledge. Of course you can research any topic you want to, but if you want to sound authoritative and do a great job, the process will be easier if you choose a topic you know than it would be if you were starting from scratch.

If you have had a long career in a particular industry – and have some credentials to back up your authority – then choosing a niche where your career experience and authority can help you to write and market your book makes a lot of sense. People are far more likely to buy and read a book from someone they perceive to be an authority than from someone who has no authority. When you play to your strengths, you increase the chances that your book will turn into a steady stream of passive income.

One thing that can be helpful in terms of choosing a niche topic is to start with a general topic and look at the sub-niches listed on the Amazon Kindle store. When you go to the Kindle Store and scroll down, you will see a list of general categories on the left-hand side of the page. Pick any topic from that list, and you will see a list of sub-categories, or niches, under it. Those sub-categories may break down further. The more specialized your chosen topic is, the easier it will be for you to attain bestseller status on Amazon. Being able to put the "Amazon Bestseller" logo on your website can do a great deal to boost sales and your perceived authority – something that can help you in other areas of passive income, too.

To get an idea of what I mean, let's look at a list of sub-niches related to a single topic on Amazon, Business and Money:

< Kindle eBooks
  Business & Money
    Accounting (15,021)
    Biography & History (13,575)
    Business Life (72,501)
    Economics (45,015)
    Education & Reference (18,314)
    Entrepreneurship & Small
    Business (87,713)
    Finance (14,174)
    Green Business (877)
    Industries (18,216)
    International (8,515)
    Investing (14,659)
    Job Hunting & Careers (12,657)
    Management &
    Leadership (61,126)
    Marketing & Sales (34,913)
    Organizational Behavior (8,023)
    Personal Finance (9,859)
    Real Estate (6,043)
    Skills (24,401)
    Taxation (1,835)
    Technology (13,029)
    Women & Business (4,215)

Clicking on the first niche, Accounting, reveals another list of six sub-niches, including auditing, governmental accounting, and managerial accounting. If you have a basic idea of the area you want to write about, looking at the list of sub-niches on Amazon can be a good way to narrow down your options.

It may also be helpful to look at the specific titles available in a niche and how well they are selling. Reading reviews may help you to identify a topic that is of interest to readers. For example, if several reviewers mention that they wish an author had covered a particular topic in more depth, you might want to consider writing a book about that topic.

Even if you are planning to hire a ghostwriter, you need to pick a niche and topic for your book. You are going to have to market the book, so you will still need to do some basic research and learn a bit about the niche in question. It is also not a bad idea to provide the writer with an outline or – at the very least – a list of topics you want to be covered in your book. I'll talk more about that later in the chapter.

Writing the Book vs. Hiring a Ghostwriter

The next decision you have to make is whether to write the book yourself or hire a ghostwriter to do it for you. Let's take a minute to look at the some of the benefits of each option, starting with writing the book yourself:

- If you write the book yourself, you do not have to pay a ghostwriter. The only investment you need to make is your time and creativity.

- Writing the book yourself guarantees that you have full creative control over the content. When you turn research over to a ghostwriter, you are taking the chance that certain topics may not be covered in the way you want them to be – and that may require an additional investment on your part depending on the nature of your agreement with the writer you hire.

- A book you write yourself will reflect your true voice, and if you are writing about a topic that you feel passionately about, your passion will come through in the writing. A ghostwriter will do their best to emulate the tone you specify, but the book may not sound like you.

- Marketing a book that you have written yourself may come more naturally than marketing a book written by a ghostwriter. You will be able to talk about your book with a great deal of passion and authority because you will be familiar with every aspect of it in a way that only the person who wrote it can be.

Now let's look at the benefits of hiring a ghostwriter:

- Your time is valuable. While you will have to pay to have your book ghostwritten, the amount that it costs you in dollars may be inexpensive compared to the amount of time it would take you to write the book yourself, especially if you are not particularly comfortable writing.

- When you hire a ghostwriter who is knowledgeable about your chosen niche, you are getting two things -- a professional writer and researcher -- for the price of one. A lot of professional writers specialize in a particular niche or area, and the fact that they write about a topic all the time can be a real benefit to you, especially if you want your book to be about a topic that is not something you know a lot about.

- If you write the book yourself, you may need to consider hiring a professional copy editor and/or proofreader to ensure that your book is properly punctuated and free of grammatical and spelling errors. A professional ghostwriter should take care of those things for you as part of their regular service and deliver a professional book with proper grammar.

As you can see, there are pros and cons to each option. I recommend hiring a ghostwriter if you are very uncomfortable writing or if you struggle with proper English. A lot of people who hire ghostwriters speak English as a second language and want to ensure that the book that has their name on it is properly written.

Tips for Writing a Book

Let's start with the writing. A lot of people don't think of themselves as writers, but the truth is that writing is just putting words together in a meaningful way. That's something you do all day, every day, whether you are composing Tweets, talking on the phone, or replying to an email. A book is just a longer version of that.

To give you an idea of how easy it can be to get an eBook up on Amazon, let me share with you the fact that the average book on the Kindle Store is only about 10,000 words long. That translates to somewhere in the vicinity of 32-40 pages of text. That's not much at all. If you wrote as little as 500 words per day, you could have a draft of your book in less than three weeks.

If writing is something that doesn't come easily to you, it may help to come up with a detailed outline first. Looking at the tables of contents in other books in your chosen niche is a good way to get ideas about what to include. You don't have to buy the books unless you want to. Many Kindle titles have a "Look Inside" feature that will let you read the table of contents and the first chapter or so of the book. That may be enough to give you a feel for what you want to include.

If you are very uncomfortable with the idea of writing, you may want to consider using a speech-to-text tool. The benefit of doing that is that you don't have to write, at least not at first. You can pick a topic, talk about it, and let the tool you use translate it into text. You will still have to review the text, correct errors, and work to create a good flow with your content, but the process itself can be easy. Oftentimes, it is easier for someone who doesn't consider themselves to be a writer to work with something that is already written than it is to feel like they have to start from scratch with a blank page.

When you have a first draft written, I strongly suggest that you put it away for a week or two before attempting to revise it. Having some time away from your project can help you look at it with a fresh perspective. When you do bring it out again, reading it out loud is a very good way to spot repeated words and awkward phrasing. When we read silently, our eyes tend to skip words. Reading out loud is also an effective way to proofread and spot homonym usage and other common mistakes.

Once you have revised the book, you should hire a professional editor or proofreader if you think your book may still contain errors. There is no shame in getting another pair of eyes on your book. It may also be helpful to get some people who are knowledgeable about your topic to read the book and give their opinions.

Tips for Hiring a Ghostwriter

If you don't feel that you want to write a book yourself, you have the option of hiring a ghostwriter to write the book for you. Ghostwriters are widely available on sites such as www.outsource.com and www.freelancer.com. The key thing to keep in mind is that you want to make sure that you are hiring someone who is a good writer, ideally one who is knowledgeable about your niche. Here are some tips to help you choose the right ghostwriter.

1. Write a detailed job description for the project you have in mind. You don't have to include your outline or list of topics, but you should give an indication of what general topic your book will cover, how long you want it to be, how quickly you expect the project to be completed, and how much you are willing to pay. You don't have to specify

an exact amount, but it is a good idea to give a range. Keep in mind that if your price is very low, you run the risk of attracting sub-par writers.

2. Specify any qualifications that you expect bidding writers to have. For example, you might want to say that you want only native English speakers to apply, and that you prefer a writer who is experienced writing about your chosen niche. You should also ask for a writing sample. Some sites don't allow writers to attach a sample to their initial bid. In those cases, you should request samples from the writers whose bids appeal most to you.

3. Narrow your list down by reading bids and samples, and requesting samples as needed. As you evaluate samples, keep in mind the tone that you want your book to have. Do you prefer a casual and conversational tone, or a more formal one? A skilled ghost-writer may be able to emulate many different tones, but if you find a writer whose voice is particularly appealing to you, that may be a deciding factor.

4. After you have narrowed your list based on writing samples, it's time to interview writers. Unless you are hiring a writer through an eBook publisher with a stellar reputation,

you should not skip this step. The reason is that many of the people bidding on your job may be from countries where English is not the primary language. In certain cases, writers may take samples that they have not written and use them to get a job. When you speak to a writer directly, it is easy to get a good idea of whether they can write. As I mentioned earlier, writing is simply stringing words together. A person who cannot speak using proper English will most likely be unable to use proper English when writing.

5. Finally, make your decision and hire the writer you want. You should agree upon a price and timeframe. Most of the freelancing websites out there make it possible for you to set up your payments to the writer in advance. A professional writer will insist upon it, as there are unscrupulous people out there who might not do that and then refuse to pay the writer. You should be prepared to fund the project. The money will be held on account until the writer has completed the job and you have approved their work. You should also make sure to specify what you expect in terms of rewriting as needed. If you are paying an hourly rate, you have to be prepared to pay more for additional work. If not, you should come to an agreement

about how much rewriting is included in your price.

I recommend the same methods you would use for a book you wrote yourself when it comes to finalizing the book. Read it out loud, and make detailed notes about any changes you want made to the book. You have the option of asking the writer to make changes, or making them yourself.

Creating a Cover

The next thing you have to consider when creating an eBook is the cover. The saying is that you shouldn't judge a book by its cover, but the truth is that many people do. Even if you choose a very small and specialized niche, your book will be competing against dozens – if not hundreds – of others in the Kindle store. You need to make sure that your cover stands out in a crowd.

Unless you have experience in graphic design, I strongly recommend hiring a professional designer to craft your cover. If you use a ghostwriter hired through an eBook publisher, they may include a cover design in the quoted price. If not, you will have to go out and hire someone yourself. You can hire freelance designers on Freelancer. Another very inexpensive choice is to post the job on Fiverr. Fiverr is a website where you can hire freelancers to do jobs for as little as five dollars – in fact, most jobs listed there are five dollars. If you search for eBook covers, you will come up with a list of people who are willing to design a cover.

When choosing a designer, use some of the same methods you would to hire a ghostwriter. Ask to see samples of their past work. You should give some thought to the style of cover you want. If there are particular images or colors you want used, you need to specify those as well. It is a good idea to choose someone who has experience designing covers for Kindle books. Keep in mind that you want your cover image to look good at full size and as a thumbnail, since that is how it will display on the Kindle store.

I strongly recommend that you look at the other covers in your niche before designing a cover or hiring a designer. Pay special attention to the bestsellers. What is it about those covers that appeals to you? Make notes and use existing covers as examples to give the designer an idea of what you want.

Formatting Your Book for Kindle

Once you have your book written and a cover designed, the next step is to format your book for the Kindle store. The instructions for Kindle Direct Publishing (KDP), which you can find on https://kdp.amazon.com/help?topicId=A17W8UM0 MMSQX6, should be relatively easy to follow if you are familiar with Microsoft Word. If you use another word processing software, you may need to transfer the file to Word to format it properly.

The main things to remember as you are formatting your book is that you must insert page breaks at the end of every chapter to ensure a smooth reading experience. Kindle readers expect books to be formatted in a certain way, and if the chapters run together you may end up with complaints about the formatting.

I also recommend taking the time to put in bookmarks to give the book a navigable table of contents. Put your table of contents where Amazon specifies, after the copyright page and before the rest of your content. From there, you can use Word's automatic tool to create a table of contents or create one manually. You should also take the time to insert bookmarks so that readers can navigate to the beginning of the book and the table of contents from anywhere in the book. The instructions on how to do that are on the Kindle formatting page I linked to earlier in the section.

Tips for Writing a Great Book Description

The final thing you need to consider before uploading your book to the Kindle store is writing a great book description that will help sell your book. If you hired a ghostwriter, then I recommend paying the same person a little extra to write a book description too – or including the book description in your original job description and ne-negotiating the price accordingly.

Remember that the description should not be a book report. You don't want a dry and serious recap of what's in the book. There's an old advertising adage about selling the sizzle, not the steak. Your description should sizzle. In other words, you want to accurately describe your book in a way that makes it seem positively irresistible.

To do that, keep your focus on what benefits readers can expect to get from your book as opposed to telling them how great your book is. By the time they are done reading your description, you want them to feel as if NOT buying your book would be a mistake.

A good book description should have plenty of white space to make it easy to read. Break your content up into short paragraphs, and use bullet points, too. You should also make sure to:

- Choose keywords (Amazon lets you choose up to seven)

- Use the same keywords in your book description

- Use formatting options to make your headline stands out. For example:

- <b> to make your headline bold </b>

- <i> to italicize your text </i>

- <h1> your headline text </h1>

- <h2> the Amazon orange headline, which appears as the subheading </h2>

- Choose categories (niches and sub-niches) to help Amazon know where to list your book

Using these simple formatting options and writing tips can make your Amazon book description sing.

Uploading Your Book on KDP

Once you have written a great book description, it's time to upload your book using KDP. You will start by visiting the KDP home page www.kdp.amazon.com, and creating a new account. From there, you will enter your book details, including your title, keywords, and categories as outlined above.

After that, you will upload your word file to KDP. Again, the preferred format is Word but there are instructions https://kdp.amazon.com/help?topicId=A14LJ3QN DNO64G on how to upload and format an HTML,

TXT, or PDF file. Once you upload the file, KDP will convert it to the proper format so it can be read on a Kindle.

The final step in uploading your book is to set a price and specify the rights for the book. Most books for sale on the Kindle Store sell for $9.99 or less, and it's a good idea to keep that in mind when pricing your book. If your book is very short, then you may want to consider pricing it lower than that. Amazon does retain the right to reprice your book based on the pricing of other books in your category.

You will also need to choose your royalty level. Amazon offers two options, 70% and 35%. Books that are in the public domain must be priced at the 35% level, but since you are writing an original, you can choose the 70% option

Keep in mind that you can also use Amazon's CreateSpace site to print hard copies of your book if you want them. If you choose to do that, you will want to review Amazon's pricing guidelines above to make sure the price for your Kindle book makes sense when viewed in relation to hard copies of your book.

Tips for Marketing Your Book

The final topic I want to cover in this chapter is the issue of marketing your book. The only way to turn your new eBook into a reliable stream of passive income is to do some promotions to get people to buy your book. Here are some suggestions:

- If you have the resources to do it and don't mind spending a bit of money, you might consider filming a book trailer and posting it on YouTube. I'll cover YouTube in detail later in the book, but a book trailer is a short video, usually two minutes or less, that serves as a commercial for your book. Think of it as the book version of a movie trailer. If you decide to make a trailer, your goal should be to make the book sound as compelling as possible.

- Do you have a blog? If so, your blog is the perfect place to publicize your new book. You can build anticipation for its release by blogging about your writing process and announcing the release date. You might consider giving out some free copies of the book by hosting a contest. One good way to do that is to offer a free entry to everybody who comments on your blog, and then offer additional entries to readers who share information about your contest on Facebook, Twitter, and other social media sites. Your readers earn additional chances to win your book, and you win a ton of free publicity.

- I also highly recommend advertising your book on social media. For example, you might set up a page for your book on Facebook, and then create an ad that targets the people you think are most likely to read your book. You will have to spend some time considering your target audience. You also have the option of targeting your Facebook connections and their friends, but only do that if you think those people represent a likely audience for your book. Otherwise, you are better off sticking to your target demographics and simply asking your friends to share information about your book. You might also want to consider a sponsored Tweet or Pin (Pinning your book cover on Pinterest is a great way to get the word out).

- Another good idea is to reach out to key authority figures and influencers in your niche and ask them to read and review your book. You may want to give out free copies to influential bloggers or people who have a huge social media following. If your book is well-reviewed, the fact that you gave a copy away won't hurt you in terms of income.

Pay attention to your Amazon sales, and read reviews to get ideas about how to improve and update your content. It is important to remain respectful (and not defensive) if you choose to re-reply directly to reviewers. Remember that you don't have to take every suggestion they make. Look at your reviews for ideas, and encourage people you know to read and review the book, too.

If you follow the guidelines in this chapter and start today, you could have your first eBook up on the Amazon Kindle store within a month or two. I know the process might seem daunting, but in my opinion, it is well worth the time and effort required. In fact, this is my favorite passive income method – and that's why I've dedicated so many pages to the topic.

In the next chapter, I will talk about my second favorite passive income method – marketing affiliate products.

Chapter 4: Marketing Affiliate Products

Perhaps writing an eBook doesn't appeal to you. Now it's time to talk about an alternative, one that – once again – will require some effort and cost to set up but can end up earning you income for years to come if you do it properly.

If you have spent any time at all learning about earning money online, you have undoubtedly heard about affiliate marketing. In case you haven't, let me briefly explain. Affiliate marketing involves marketing products (usually by putting links on your blog or website) that were created by other people. In exchange for displaying the ads, you get a percentage of the sales that happen as a result. Sometimes you may get paid only if there is a sale, while other affiliate offers may aim at generating leads and pay you for each person who clicks on the ad.

Let's walk through what you need to do to successfully market affiliate products. Just as was the case with writing an eBook, it all starts with choosing the right niche.

Choosing a Niche

Many of the same issues apply to choosing a niche to sell affiliate products that apply to choosing a niche for an eBook. I'm not going to waste your time by repeating the same content, so if you skipped the last chapter, I recommend going back to read the section about niche selection.

What I would like to add is that if you already have a blog in a particular niche, adding niche products to the blog can be a relatively quick and easy way to set up passive streams of income. A blog, especially if you already have a sizeable following, is a great marketing tool. Each post you write uses keywords and covers a topic in your chosen niche. If you decide to put affiliate links on your blog, you can review the products you decide to sell and link to your opt-in or sales page from the review itself in addition to posting the affiliate ads on your site.

If you don't have a blog already but there is a niche that appeals to you, starting one is a very good first step when it comes to marketing affiliate products. Blogging can help you establish yourself as an authority figure in your chosen niche, which will give your choice of certain products more weight than it would have otherwise.

I do recommend sticking with products in a single niche as you get started. You can always branch out to other, related niches as you get things established. However, as a new affiliate marketer you don't want to overdo it. You are going to have to spend some time creating content (or hiring someone to create it), as well as setting up and testing an effective sales funnel. The narrower your specialty is, the easier it will be to build upon your knowledge and start the money flowing.

Checking out the Competition

Another good preliminary step when marketing affiliate products is to do some basic keyword research. A keyword is any word or series of words that an internet user types into a search engine. Looking at keyword usage and trends can help you identify topics within a niche that get a high volume of search traffic – in other words, they can help you narrow down your choice of products to those that have the best chance of selling.

One tool that I like to use is Market Samurai, which lets you view the top trending keywords in any niche. When you sign up for a free membership, you also get access to videos that will provide you with valuable information about how to tell the difference between a truly valuable keyword and one that might get high traffic but never earn you any money.

It's also a good idea to search for the top blogs in your chosen niche and see which affiliate products they are promoting. You can start by doing a

Google search for "your niche" + blogs. I recom-recommend looking at the top ten blogs that show up and writing down the names of the products they sell. That can provide you with a good jumping off point to research products.

Researching Products

Once you have a niche, some high-traffic keywords, and a list of potential products to promote, it's time to research those products and find out whether they are worth promoting. The site that I recommend for product research is www.clickbank.com, a massive marketplace where you can check out affiliate products and learn about them. ClickBank is free to use and is a great resource to look up information about the products you found earlier and find new ones, too.

For each product listed on their site, ClickBank provides a series of statistics to help you learn about them. For example, you can learn:

- Init $/sale tells you how much you would make for the sale of a product.

- Avg Rebill Total applies only to products that bill on a recurring basis, such as membership sites and subscriptions.

- Avg $/sale is the same as the initial sale for one-time products, but will include the average rebill for products that include that option.

- Avg %/sale tells you what the average commission percentage is for all products (including rebills and upsells) for a particular product

- Rebill %/sale tells you the commission you can expect to earn for rebills.

- Grav is a unique statistic created by ClickBank to tell you how hot a particular product is. It is a reflection of recent sales as well as the number of affiliates promoting a product, so a high Grav number might make a product a good choice, but may also indicate that you will have a significant amount of competition.

When you click on a category or subcategory on ClickBank, you will see the products listed in order of popularity. However, you can also choose to sort the products by any one of the statistics provided to get an idea of which products you prefer.

I recommend taking a look at the top products in your chosen category and also looking up the products you noted earlier. Narrow them down based on what you learn. After that, I recommend taking the following steps to thoroughly research the products left on your list:

1. Do a Google search and read reviews of the product. You're going to face an uphill battle if you choose to promote a product that has a slew of bad reviews, and you might as well know about it up front. If you notice a lot of complaints or people saying they have returned the product for a refund, you may want to think twice about sinking your time and effort into marketing it.

2. Opt in to the mailing list for each product so you can get an idea of what the sales funnel is like. You want to know what materials you're going to get as an affiliate.

3. Do a search for affiliates who sell the product in question. You should look for complaints from affiliates, especially those

that have to do with not getting paid in a timely manner. You may also want to reach out to marketers in your niche to see what they have to say about a particular product. Knowledge is power.

4. Once you have narrowed down your list again to three or four products, I strongly suggest that you buy at least the basic product to see what it's like. Trust me, you don't want to be selling a product that you know nothing about. You need to know what is included with purchase of the product so you understand what you will be selling. Doing a thorough review of the product can help you make your final decision and see what's worth selling and what isn't. Many products have a 30-day money back guarantee, so you can always return a product that you think is no good for a refund.

By the time you are done with your research, you should have a product (or maybe more than one) that you feel you can do a good job promoting. The more strongly you believe in a product, the easier it will be to promote it. If you're selling a product you haven't seen and don't understand, your lack of knowledge is going to show – especially if you are promoting it on social media and on your blog.

Some of the best products to sell include digital products such as eBooks and online courses. They pay high commissions – sometimes as much as 50% -- and they are a fairly easy sell. Another good option is to market memberships in online forums and membership sites, which can set you up to receive recurring commissions if people buy ongoing memberships. I also like to look for a product that has a good number of upsells. For example, many basic weight loss plans have upsells that include:

- Cookbooks

- Food measurement cups and accessories

- Fitness programs

- Workout DVDs

The more upsells and related products there are, the higher your earning potential is. Look at the entire sales funnel of a product before you select it so you understand exactly what product(s) you will be promoting.

Set Up a Page Using WordPress

Once you have chosen a product to promote, the next step is to set up a landing page using WordPress. WordPress is free software that you can use to design an effective website even if you have no design experience or programming knowledge. All of the programming is accom-accomplished from a user-friendly dashboard that makes setting up a landing page for your new affiliate product a snap.

If you already have a blog, you may already be familiar with WordPress, since it is the most popular software to use to set up a blog. If you're new to WordPress, I want to clarify that I am talking about WordPress.org, not WordPress.com. WordPress.com is a free blogging site, but it is not the same as having your own website. To effectively market affiliate products, you must have your own site. Many affiliate programs require affiliates to own their own domain name.

You have the option of hosting your site through WordPress directly, or of using another host. Most hosts allow the use of WordPress. I caution you against choosing a free or very cheap hosting program. What you save in up-front costs can come back to haunt you in the form of excessive downtime and poor customer service.

Choose a domain name that relates to the product you are selling. Ideally, you want to use some of the most popular keywords you found while you were researching. If a product is sold by many of your competitors, finding a great domain name may prove to be a challenge. If a .com name isn't available, consider using one of the other extensions such as .biz or .us instead.

When you set up your site on WordPress, you can choose from hundreds of free themes. I strong suggest that you choose a mobile-responsive theme. As of 2015, more people conduct searches on mobile devices than on computers. Google penalizes sites that are not mobile-friendly, so there is no reason to choose anything other than a mobile-responsive theme for your new site.

Here are some other things to keep in mind when setting up your new landing page:

- Write a strong headline that indicates what people can expect to see on the page and creates a strong desire to keep reading. Try to use your primary keyword in the headline.

- Choose a theme that is eye-catching but not unpleasant to look at. Clashing colors may actually drive people away from your site. You want them to stay, read or watch your content, and OPT IN. If your site is too garish it may have the opposite effect.

- Stay away from fancy fonts that are difficult to read. It's fine to use a special font here and there for emphasis, but do not choose something that is overly ornate.

- Consider making a sales video for your page. There is evidence to show that landing pages with videos tend to get more conversions than pages without video. You can provide the video content in written form as an alternative for people who prefer not to watch a video.

- If you choose to have only written content on your page, make sure that it is well-written and compelling. Everything you write (or pay to have written) should focus on solving a particular problem that the person reading your page has – and explain how the product you're promoting can help them solve it. Break up the content with subheadings and bullet points to make it easy to read.

- Focus on creating natural-sounding content to improve your Google rank. Simply using your keywords over and over again isn't enough these days. Your content must be relevant and compelling, and your use of keywords must be natural and not forced.

- Choose a strong call to action that repeats multiple times on the page. The best CTAs are those that emphasize the benefits of using the product you are selling. For example:

    o Lose Weight NOW

    o Yes, I want to retire early

o Help me train my dog

All of these are solution oriented and far more appealing than a bland "Click here."

Optimizing Your Site

Setting up your basic website is important, but you also want to do whatever you can to ensure that your site is fully optimized. I could write an entire book about SEO, but my goal here is simply to give you an overview so you make sure to hit the important points.

- Your landing page should be optimized for one main keyword and several secondary keywords. Your primary keyword should be a long-tail keyword – one that is very specific and tailored to people who are ready to spend money to solve the problem that your chosen product addresses.

- Do not worry about keyword density. As mentioned before, the most important thing is the quality of your content. Use your keywords in your headline, in the first sentence of your content, and in a few other prominent locations.

- Don't neglect your tags and descriptions. The information that appears on your page is only half the battle when it comes to SEO.

You should also use your keywords in the following places:

- Your page title (the title that appears when your page comes up in response to a Google search)
- Your meta description (the short description that appears under your page title on Google)
- Your H1 and H2 tags, which let Google know where your headlines and subheadings are
- Your alt, or image tags, which appear when one of your images fails to properly download on a viewer's page

Using these tags properly can do a great deal to boost your SEO.

Everything on your page should be informative and relevant to people who are searching your chosen keywords. While keywords and tags are important, Google places the highest premium on content that is well-written and relevant. As long as your page has high-quality content and uses keywords effectively, you should do well on Google.

Market on Social Media

One of my favorite ways to market affiliate products is on social media. Unlike advertising with Google AdWords, social media advertising is still relatively inexpensive. You can buy an ad on Facebook for as little as five dollars per day. Unlike search engine advertising, which relies on keyword usage, social media ads allow you to target people based on two categories of information:

- Demographics, including age range, gender, income level, and geographical location

- Psychographics, including buying habits, hobbies, and interests

If you set up a business page for your affiliate product, you can use it to share relevant content and place ads. Facebook advertising is the most well-established of all the social media websites. Here are some other benefits of using Facebook to market your affiliate products:

- Facebook offers you the option to manage an unlimited number of pages from your primary account. If you are marketing more than one affiliate product, you can easily set up a page for each.

- You can follow publications and pages that are relevant to your niche and use them to find and share content with your followers.

- Facebook has a free scheduling tool that you can use to set up posts in advance.

- You'll have access to Facebook Insights, which provides you with analytics to determine how your page is performing and which posts get the most engagement.

When you place an ad with Facebook, you can send the people who click on it directly to your new landing page. Each week, you'll get an email from Facebook showing how your ad has performed so you can tweak it and revisit it as needed.

Of course, Facebook is not the only social media site you can use to promote your affiliate products. Here are some others to consider:

- Twitter is still very popular and its 140-character limit makes it a good choices for sending out quick facts and promotions. At present, the only way to advertise on Twitter is with a sponsored Tweet. Sponsoring increases the chances that your Tweet will be seen by all of your followers.
- Pinterest is a hugely effective tool for marketing affiliate products, especially if the product you are selling is aspirational or appeals strongly to women. Pinterest users tend to be fairly affluent and are far more likely to make purchases based on what

they see on the site than people on other social media sites. Pinterest recently opened up its advertising options to all businesses.

- Snapchat is a relatively new social media site and one that appeals strongly to young people. If you have a following on Snapchat, you can use it to send out quick announcements and things of that nature as a way of informing people about your product.
- Instagram is highly visual and now offers paid advertising. If the product you are selling lends itself to being photographed, it can be very effective as a way of spreading the word about your product.

If you decide to use social media to market your product, you should remember to adhere to the 4-to-1 rule. For every one piece of content you post that is directly related to the product you are marketing, you should post four that are related to your niche and provide value to your followers without mentioning your product. Remember, people do not follow businesses on social media because they want to be bombarded with an endless string of sales pitches. They want to be informed and entertained.

Creating Backlinks for Better SEO

The final topic I want to mention relates to SEO. When we discussed SEO earlier, we focused on on-site SEO – the things you can do on your website that will help it achieve a high rank on Google when people search your chosen keywords. However, there is another element to SEO, and that has to do with getting other websites to link back to your site.

The best backlinks to get are from high-quality, authority sites in your chosen niche. It is possible to buy backlinks, but that is considered a "black hat" SEO tactic and I don't recommend it. If you get caught, Google can penalize you. Instead, focus on contacting bloggers and publications in your niche. Write guest blogs and articles, list your site in niche directories, and make sure to encourage friends and other people who have websites to link to your site whenever possible.

It takes time to accumulate quality backlinks, but it's worth the time and effort. The more links you have, the higher the volume of traffic you will get to your landing page.

One final note regarding affiliate marketing. If you are marketing affiliate products on your blog, you don't want your blog to appear overly cluttered or spammy, either to your visitors or to Google. One way to keep things under control is to do some of your affiliate marketing via email. If you get people to sign up for your email list, you can market individual products to them in an email without in-including a link on your site. The same is true of short, free eBooks. The benefit of both methods is that you are providing your subscribers and visitors with something free (an informative email or book) and that means they are far more likely to buy what you suggest than they would be if you simply presented them with a hard sales pitch.

Chapter 5: Other Passive Income Methods

While writing eBooks and marketing affiliate products are my two favorite methods of earning passive income, they are certainly not the only methods to use. In this chapter, I will cover several other methods that you may want to consider, and give you an overview of each. I recommend that you read through the chapter and see which ideas appeal to you the most. You can then move forward with your chosen ideas and work toward setting them up so they generate passive income.

How to Create and Market a Mobile App

It used to be that creating an app to sell was considered overly risky. For marketers who lacked programming experience, it meant hiring a programmer to design and create the app, and that usually translated to prohibitive up-front costs. However, that's changed now – and if you do it right, creating and selling an app can be a good way to earn passive income.

Creating an App Concept

If you already have a great idea for an app and you have the wherewithal to create it, then I encourage you to do it. It's always going to be a bit of a crapshoot, but if you take the time to market it on your blog or on social media, you might be able to sell enough copies to earn a steady stream of income. You probably already know that places like the Apple Store and the Google Store sell apps, and you can now buy apps on the Amazon App Store as well.

What can you do if you don't have an idea for an app? One solution that I like to suggest is piggybacking on an existing app. What I mean is that you can look at popular apps in your niche and figure out a way to put a twist on them. Let's look at an example of an app that found a way to offer something new in an overcrowded niche. The weight loss app Lose It offers some features that make it stand out from the other weight loss apps that are available. It allows users to use their smart phones to scan bar codes to get calorie counts of packaged foods. It saves every item you scan, as well as individual meals so you can find them easily. It also allows simple look-up of meals at popular restaurants, including fast food and sit-down options.

If you can find a way to take a popular app and put a new spin on it by adding additional features or approaching things from a new angle, you might be able to earn a nice stream of passive income by marketing your app.

Creating Your App

The next step is to create your app. If you have extensive programming experience, you can certainly create and program the app yourself. However, as a rule I do not recommend trying to create the app yourself. You can hire a programmer on many of the same sites that I mentioned earlier, including places like www.freelancer.com and www.upwork.com. Of course you will have to pay out some money up front, but once you do you can hand over the work to a programmer. You'll need to explain exactly what you want the app to do. I recommend making a complete list of the functionalities you want included. Give some thought to whether you want to allow in-app purchases and things of that nature. A good programmer should have a list of questions that will help you narrow down what you want.

You also have the option of using online resources to create the app yourself if that is your preference. Here are two that I like:

www.appypie.com – a website that provides the tools to help you create your own mobile app www.zapporoo.com – another mobile app creation resource

Marketing Your App

Once you have a completed app that's tested and ready to sell, you can sell it on the places I mentioned earlier, including the Apple Store, the Google Store, and the Amazon App Store. However, you should also do some marketing of your own. I strongly recommend that you set up a WordPress site to sell your app directly to consumers, using the same tips that I listed in the last chapter about affiliate marketing.

You should also consider setting up social media sites to market your app. You can include screen shots that show people what the app can do. As you collect testimonials, you can add them to your WordPress page and list them on your social media pages too.

Creating a mobile app isn't for everybody, but if you have a great idea and the willingness to pay somebody to program the app for you, it can be a good way to set up a passive income stream.

How to Create and Monetize a YouTube Channel

Sometimes, new marketers get scared off by the thought of making videos. I know that filming your own videos can seem intimidating, and you might imagine that it would be prohibitively expensive as well. However, the opposite is actually true. You need very little in the way of technical expertise to film a video, and if you're comfortable talking off the cuff you don't even need to write a formal script.

With that in mind, let's talk about how making videos and posting them on your own YouTube channel can help earn you money. Videos are one of the most popular forms of online content. In fact, most people would prefer to watch a short (two or three minute) video to reading a couple of short blog posts, even though the time invested would be approximately the same.

Videos tend to be shared on social media far more frequently than other forms of content – in fact, they're more popular than written content and photographs combined. That means that once you create a video, it can spread with very little effort required on your part.

How to Create a YouTube Channel

Creating a YouTube channel is very easy. If you have a Gmail or Google+ account, you can use your ID to log in to YouTube. Once you are logged in, you can simply click your profile picture at the top right-hand corner of the screen and choose the "Create Channel" option to create your channel.

Copyright © 2016 Ralph Waters

When you create your channel, you should make sure to do all of the following;

- Create a channel name that reflects your niche and the kind of content you will be posting

- Choose a profile picture or logo that is unique and memorable. If you are using your name, then it's a good idea to use the same photograph you use on your social media accounts to give some continuity to your online presence

- Write a keyword-rich description of your channel that includes a link back to your website and gives viewers an accurate idea of what they can expect to find on your channel

Because YouTube is owned by Google, there are some great SEO benefits to using YouTube. I'll talk a bit more about those in a minute.

Tips for Creating Memorable Videos

As I mentioned before, you don't need a ton of technical expertise to create video content. Your goal should be to create videos that provide both entertainment and value to your target audience. Here are some potential ideas for marketing videos:

- Tell a short story that highlights a key topic in your niche or explains a product you are marketing

- Create a whiteboard or animated video that helps to explain a complicated concept relevant to your niche

- Make an entertaining product demo or product unboxing video that highlights one or your affiliate products

- Do a viewer Q & A where you solicit questions from your social media followers or in the comments section of your YouTube videos

Just as you did with your eBook, you can hire a professional writer to come up with a video script if you are not comfortable speaking off the cuff.

Ways to Monetize Your Videos

Now let's talk about how your videos earn money on YouTube. The easiest way to do it is to opt-in to the AdSense option. AdSense runs ads before your video, giving users an opportunity to click to buy a product. The benefit of using AdSense here is that, if you do a video on a particular technical topic, the ad that pops up will likely be something relevant to your niche. Users are very likely to click on relevant ads if they feel your video has been helpful, and you will earn a commission eve-every time they do.

Keep in mind that AdSense is not going to make you rich. However, using YouTube can be a very good way to create a new passive income stream without having to spend a lot of money or time.

Another option is to create a video series and require users to pay to watch it. Since most videos on YouTube are free, you will have to be fairly confident that people will be willing to pay for your content. We'll talk about online courses in a minute, but creating a webinar or video course is certainly an option for YouTube.

How to Promote Your Videos

It is important to keep in mind that YouTube is one of the world's most-trafficked websites. In fact, it's also the world's second-largest search engine after Google. It is far easier to get a YouTube video to rank for search for a particular keyword than it is to get your blog or website to rank. Google seems to favor YouTube videos in search results – probably because users favor them too. You can get a lot more attention with video than you can with other content. When you name your video and write a description for it, make sure to use your chosen keywords and take full advantage of tags, too. That will ensure that your video ranks high on Google.

I also recommend embedding your videos on your website, and sharing them with your social media contacts. Video is highly shareable and very popular, so sharing it on social media makes a lot of sense. For example, if you have a Facebook page for your affiliate products and your video is relevant to that niche, you can share it there and encourage your followers to share, it too. You can also boost the post, thus ensuring that your video will get out in front of a whole new group of fans.

How to Create an Online Course

Is there a topic that you know inside out? If you've spent years working in a particular industry or studying a particular topic, then it might be worthwhile to spend the time and energy setting up an online course.

I want to be honest about this: setting up an online course is a ton of work. You're going to have to write content, create course materials, and possibly film videos, too. It can easily take five times as long as it takes to create an eBook if you do it right – and that's a big time investment, no question.

The reason I think it's worth it is that you can earn back all of that time on the back end. It might take five times as long to set up an online course as an eBook, but you can also realistically charge five or ten times as much for it. If you charge $9.99 for your eBook, you might be able to sell a course for as much as $149.00 – a huge mark-up that allows you to rake in high income in perpetuity.

Tips for Creating a Course

The key to offering an online course is to pick a niche in which you are comfortable, one that has enough traffic to warrant the time and effort you are going to spend creating the course. One good way to do that is to do keyword research using Google AdWords or SemRush to identify long-tail keywords with a high-enough search volume to make setting up a class worthwhile.

Keep in mind that you do have the option, again, of outsourcing certain elements of your course creation. You can hire a writer to write video scripts for you, as well as to write or edit course materials. If you plan on using video, it may be worthwhile to hire a professional videographer to ensure that your videos look polished. Many online teachers charge a great deal of money for courses. If you want to be able to do the same you must make sure that your students feel they are getting what they paid for.

Tips for Marketing Your Online Course

The first thing to consider is where you will make your course available. Sites like www.udemy.com and www.teachable.com are good options because they are well known sources of online education. You will have to pay a small percentage of your sales price in return for listing your course there. I think it's worth the expense. People are far more likely to search for an online course on those sites than they are to head to Google.

You may also want to consider the following methods of publicizing your course:

- Setting up a WordPress site and sales funnel to direct people to your course

- Creating social media ads to send people to your pages on Udemy, or to your WordPress site

- Setting up a Facebook page to promote your course – you can share tidbits from the class and even post excerpts from some of your course videos if you want to

- Send previews of your course to key influencers in your niche and ask them to review or recommend the course to their followers.

- Another thing to consider when it comes to setting up an online course is whether you can leverage it into a source of recurring income. One way to do that is to set up a website with a private discussion forum. Af- After people take the class, you can offer them a membership plan with the promise that you will provide them with things such as:

- Updates on the course materials

- New resources related to your niche

- Access to members-only forums and exclusive information

- Mentoring with you

- Exclusive Q & A sessions with you and other experts

The benefit of spinning your course into a membership site is that if you keep your members happy, you can end up earning recurring income from them for months or even years. You'll have some attrition, as every membership site does, but the benefits far outweigh the risks.

Setting Up Review or Comparison Sites

The overwhelming majority of people who buy products online read product reviews and comparisons before making a purchase. In fact, research shows that 80% of all consumers won't make a purchase without reading reviews, and that they give as much credence to reviews from strangers as they would to those from people whom they know personally.

That statistic points the way to a strong money-making opportunity that can provide a legitimate service to people by giving them honest reviews of products in a particular niche. Here's how you do it:

1. Set up a website for a particular niche, and take the time to create some useful content, including blog posts, how-to videos, tutorials, and more.

2. Research some of the various products in the niche, and sign up for Amazon's affiliate program on https://affiliate-program.amazon.com/

3. Set up a page that offers side-by-side comparisons of products, or reviews of products. You can set up various options. For example, a website that focused on laptop computers might do reviews of the top five laptops in different categories, including business options, gaming computers, and 2-in-1 computers (laptops that convert to tablets.) Next to each review or comparison, you would include a "Buy" button that would lead to your affiliate link on Amazon.

The benefit of a site like this is that it offers people an easy way to make side-by-side comparisons – something that's hard to do on Amazon because users would have to switch between pages to try to get an idea of the differences and similarities between products. If you take the time to list features and give honest feedback about the pros and cons of each product, and pair it with a strong call to action at the end encouraging people to make a choice and click to buy, you can earn a nice income this way.

The key to setting up a comparison or review page is that the reviews you list must be real. It is not going to be enough to simply reiterate the product features as they are listed on Amazon. You need to give your customers a real look at how the product works. In an ideal world, you would try all of the products yourself. In the event that you are marketing relatively inexpensive products, like teeth-whitening products or kitchen gadgets, you may be able to do exactly that. However, if you are comparing laptops, trying all of them may prove to be tricky.

If you cannot try the products yourself, you must research them thoroughly and try to include as much information as possible about the experience of using the product in question. Reading consumer reports and Amazon reviews, as well as reviews in niche publications, is a good way to start.

I recommend using the information in the previous chapters to set up a WordPress site for your comparison page, optimize the site using your chosen keywords, and promote your page on social media and specialty sites in your niche. Because your goal is to have someone make a purchase from your page, I recommend using long-tail keywords that include words such as:

- Compare

- Comparison

- Review

- Purchase

- Best

- Top

These words will help you attract highly qualified traffic – people who are very close to the point where they are ready to make a purchase. What you are providing them is an easy to way to compare products without having to toggle back and forth between different sites or pages. Convenience is important, and your site can be the solution to someone's comparison-shopping problem.

The downside here is, of course, the time it takes to set up the site and get it running. Once you have cleared that hurdle, the site should require only periodic maintenance. You should continue to post to your blog and share other information, and you will also need to update your reviews periodically as products are discontinued and new products are added.

Create Your Own Product

We already talked about selling affiliate products, but this idea takes that concept to the next level. A quick perusal of ClickBank reveals that there are thousands of digital and physical products out there that you can market as an affiliate. The thing to remember about those products is that each one of them has a product creator on the other end, someone who is earning an income from every product sold by every affiliate. It stands to reason that if affiliates are earning a nice income selling those products, the product creator is earning even more.

Imagine that you create a product – say it's a combination of an eBook with some videos, as well as a physical product such as weight loss equipment or something of the kind. You set the price of your product at $99. To begin with, you sell the product yourself using your own website. As it takes off, you make the decision to set up an affiliate program offering 50% commission for each product sold.

The benefit of doing that is that you have the potential to sell many more products than you sold on your own. All you have to do is provide your affiliates with some marketing materials. For example, you might give them:

- A landing page template

- Ad copy and images to use

- Copy to use in their email campaigns

Your affiliates have to spend their own time and money marketing your products. Yes, you have to split the purchase price with them 50/50. However, you are now doing very little marketing. If you pick up 10 affiliates, then you could (in theory, at least) be selling ten times as many products as you were before. Your overhead is lower because you're not paying for advertising. The reduced amount you make for each product you sell is more than paid for by the increased volume of sales.

Tips for Creating a Product

The first step is to conceptualize your product. We've already covered how to find a niche, and if you are going to create a product it's important to do so in a niche where you already have some knowledge and authority – that's what will make people buy from you.

One method I recommend is looking at the top products on ClickBank and looking for gaps. What things aren't being covered by the available products? Is there something that reviews of the top products mention that indicates a weakness or an opportunity? Your job is to find an opening that will allow your product to stand out from the crowd.

Once you have conceptualized your product, you will need to create it. As was the case with creating an online course, the work involved in creating and manufacturing a product can be extensive. If part of your product is an eBook, you have the option of outsourcing it to a ghostwriter if you prefer. If you are including both a digital product and a physical product, you will need to find someone to manufacture the product for you.

Tips for Marketing Your Product

When you first start selling your product, you will be selling it yourself. You can create a WordPress site, promote it on your blog, and send free samples to industry influencers to review the product. You also need to give some thought to distribution. A purely digital product can simply be downloaded from your "Thank You" page. However, a physical product will likely need to be drop-shipped from the manufacturer or from a drop-ship company. That's a complicated topic, but you can learn more about it on https://www.abetterlemonadetand.com/drop-shipping-companies/.

If your product sells well, you may want to add upgrades and improvements to it, and ultimately, consider creating an affiliate program of your own. You will have to pay affiliates a decent commission to sell your product, but the upside of doing so is that they can do the marketing and other legwork for you while you relax and collect your income.

I hope you can see the benefits of taking the time to create passive income streams. The effort you put into setting them up is relatively minor compared to the earning potential in the long-term. Even the most time-consuming options, such as creating a product or an online course, can pay you back many times over if you do a good job.

Keep in mind that it is always preferable to have your income coming from more than one place. If you create a product and the market for it vanishes, you'll be left scrambling to replace that income. If you have multiple streams of income, one can dry up and you'll still be fine. That means that you'll have the best possible scenario for prolonged financial freedom because you won't have to worry about losing your income the way you would if you worked a nine-to-five job.

Conclusion

Thank you for reading *Passive Income*. I hope that after reading this book, you are feeling excited and energized about the possibilities that earning passive income can open up for you.

As you get started setting up your first streams of passive income, I want to make a few recommendations to help you get the money flowing quickly:

- Start by picking a niche where you have some expertise and setting up a blog. Add a bit of content first, and set up a Facebook page and Twitter feed to publicize your blog.

- Research affiliate products and add them to your blog. I recommend starting with a blog and affiliate products because it's one of the quickest ways to get the money flowing. It may start slowly, but any start is a good one. You can and should take this step before giving up your day job.

- Look at what you want to do next to expand on your blog. If you love writing and have an idea for a short eBook, consider making that your next step. You can publish the book for free using the link to the Kindle Publishing platform on the resources list, and you can sell the eBook on your own site as well as on Amazon.

- From there, expand by setting up a YouTube channel, adding a review and comparison page to your website, creating an online course, or even creating a product. It's a good idea to start with some of the less labor-intensive passive income methods first so you have a base of income, and then move on to some of the more time-consuming options I have outlined for you.

- Finally, do what you can to set up recurring streams of income by offering a membership site or another recurring product. When you get to this level, you can start earning significant money without having to do very much work.

The bottom line is that earning passive income can point the way to financial freedom if you take the time to do it right. It won't be easy. You will have to be willing to put in a fair amount of work up front to get things set up, and it's important to be clear-eyed about that. However, once you get things rolling, I think you'll be amazed at how much money you can earn using the methods in this book.

I wish you the best of luck. Enjoy your financial freedom!

Publisher`s Bonus:

As a way of saying "thank you" for downloading this book, we`d like to offer you the eBook "**The daily Money Motivator**" for <u>**free**</u>.

Additionally you will get access to To Our Books When They Are Free on Amazon and Kindle!

We`re committed to giving you powerful, quality e-books to help you change your life! Our authors cover a range of topics, all designed to help you live your best life.

Simply Download it on:
https://thebookclub.leadpages.co/passive-income/

Publisher Note:

Dear Customer,

If you have time, we`d love it if you would write a short, honest review of this book. Your feedback helps us improve our books as we work very closely with our authors to provide you with quality material. Since we are small publishing company, we rely on customers like you to share their experiences with our books with other customers on Amazon. Keeping our marketing costs low helps us keep our books reasonably priced. We truly appreciate every review we get, and your comments. Reviews can be done quickly here www.amazon.com/Passive-Income-complete -building-financial-ebook/dp/B01CSTC4EK/.